To

_____

From

_____

Date

_____

Praise for *40 Rules to Help Boys Become Men*

"Some boys never grow up. Even though they become men biologically, their behavior is that of a spoiled child. Good manners and etiquette are not only vital to civilization, but on a more practical level, one's ability to acquire and keep friends, a stable family, and a job depend on one's ability to 'do unto others as you would have others do unto you.' Gregg Jackson has captured that simple, yet almost forgotten principle in his simple yet profound new book, *40 Rules to Help Boys Become Men*. Let's all hope that it becomes a runaway bestseller—the civility of our society would be better off for it!"

Mike Huckabee, Former Governor, Fox News Contributor and New York Times Best-Selling Author

"Being from the south I was taught to say, 'yes sir' and 'no ma'am,' look adults in the eye and give a firm handshake. These are just a few of the many key principles that you will learn from this book that will help any young person grow up to be a cut above the rest. You can fly with the crows or soar with the eagles. This book will help you to learn in part how to soar with eagles."

Brannon Howse, Author and Nationally Syndicated Radio Host

"*40 Rules* is a reminder to this present generation that becoming all that makes a man starts with being a boy who observes, receives, and then lives out important character, respect and strength-based practices, desiring in the end that he emerge a man of integrity, a servant and true friend to others. Gregg really focuses on the 'essentials', even though at first glance, some seem rather insignificant. What I was reminded of most after reading this book is how timeless each practice is, though some have been intentionally added to reflect today's culture. Easy to read and easy to teach...it keeps the bar high for boys, who will surely, someday, fully appreciate what they were taught. Keeps us dads in practice too. :)"

Evan Dalrymple, Principal, Cherry Hills Christian Middle School

"You can tell a lot about young men by who and what they honor as well as their manners. Gregg Jackson has given us an outline to share with our sons in helping them to become productive young men and to do life better."

J.C. Watts, Former Professional Football Player and Oklahoma Congressman

"Will this book create a refreshing resurrection of decency and decorum among today's generation of young men? I certainly pray so! And if *40 Rules* can't be used to assist in accomplishing that feat – it can't be done. Another Gregg Jackson home run! It's a shame *40 Rules* had to be written. It's a blessing to us all that Gregg Jackson prayerfully produced it. I only wish I had thought of writing this book first. A masterpiece of convicting simplicity!"

Carl Gallups, Sr. Pastor, Bestselling Author & Radio Host

"One of the casualties of the Secular Age, as philosopher Charles Taylor calls our present time, is the loss of civility. To have lost the Bible in public life is to have lost not only a literate way of thinking, but a certain way of behaving. We mostly talk about this regrettable phenomena, the loss of civility and manners, as we speak of life in the public square. Not only do partisan politics routinely violate the most elementary of manners that many of us learned on our mother's knee, but, perhaps worse, the 'common man' also, joins in the new boorish age as he lurches anonymously in the cyber shadows of social media to berate, belittle, and become the epitome of self-idolization. So many of our women, even our little girls, have been made captives of the spirit of the age, as well. In a world of selfies, modesty has become as rare as chivalry.

Yet, there is always hope! Manners and courtesy ('court' behavior before the King) has its source in the Bible. And I am thrilled to endorse the new book by Gregg Jackson, *40 Rules to Help Boys Become Men: The Lost Arts of Manners, Etiquette, and Behavior.*

As I read through Gregg's simple and simply powerful list of essential manners for young men I thought of the great tradition of this kind of book. Jonathan Edwards penned *70 Resolutions*

(1722) for his own life before he turned twenty years of age. And many are familiar with a book that used to be standard curriculum in many schools, *George Washington's Rules of Civility & Decent Behavior In Company and Conversation* (c. 1744), copied from a Jesuit guide on manners when Washington was twelve years old. Gregg Jackson's new book is not only timely, but I believe will prove to be enduring, as well.

Young Washington's final entry in his 110 rules may be the best endorsement for Gregg Jackson's book, *40 Rules to Help Boys Become Men:* 'Labor to keep alive in your breast that little spark of celestial fire called conscience.' Buying and reading this book, giving it as a gift to your son, your grandson, and other youngsters is sure way to fan that spark into a flame. How we need to see the flame of civility and good manners rekindled in our day. Thanks to Gregg Jackson and his publisher for making this book available to help us all recover the necessity of manly courtesy and decency."

Michael A. Milton, PhD, MPA, President, D. James Kennedy Institute of Reformed Leadership, Chaplain (Colonel), U.S. Army Reserve, James Ragsdale Chair of Missions and Evangelism, Erskine Theological Seminary

"A lack of manliness is plaguing our culture and if something isn't done about it our country will cease to exist as it does today. There has never been a time in our nation's history when we've needed a book like this to train boys to become men. Read this book, digest its content, and pass it on. You won't regret it."

David and Jason Benham, Best-Selling Authors of *Whatever The Cost* and *Living Among Lions*

"Gregg Jackson has done it again! Following up on *40 Things to Teach Your Children Before You Die,* he has once again hit it out of the park for us parents. With no wasted words Gregg gives us a list of rules for manhood that is so simple to impart to our young men. Dads, lets model what some may call, 'old fashioned' behavior and bring back the conduct that is truly becoming of a man."

Greg Davis, Host of Priority Talk Radio

"'Chivalry is not dead. It's just no longer required.' I coined this phrase years ago but I'm delighted that Gregg Jackson is changing all that! With so much confusion about the role of men in our society, it's no wonder so many parents are at a loss about how to bring up boys. In an age when respect and honor seem like distant and antiquated relics, how can we equip boys to pursue valor and courageously put the needs of others before their own? The transformation from boys into men requires intentional guidance, education, and good role models. As a boy grows toward manhood, it is imperative that his parents instill in him the values and character traits needed to succeed in life.

"In his book, *40 Rules To Help Boys Become Men,* Gregg Jackson helps inspire moms and dads with intentional strategies in raising the kind of boys who make an impact in their community and their world, now and for the rest of their lives. This simple yet powerful book shows us how to inspire today's generation of young boys to pursue honor, courage, and compassion while motivating them to become godly men. Changing our culture starts within our homes. When we choose to define the standard of manhood and raise the level of expectation in our families, one by one and little by little, we create a shift in society. That's why the message of Gregg's book and his passion for instilling timeless values in our boys' hearts is more than a parenting book; I hope it's a movement."

Sheila Zilinsky, Talk Show Personality and Author of *Power Prayers: Warfare That Works,* and mom of 3 wonderful sons

"A new book on good manners and etiquette? You're kidding right? Not in the least! Gregg Jackson's latest book is a salvo across the cultural bow of the USS America. Our age can be characterized by many things but one that is glaring in its absence is that of a social respect and kindness toward other people. It is time to reengage American society with a reminder that all this talk about respecting people is so much hot air unless actually put into practice. Parents, it is time to once again take seriously the importance of rearing your children to honor and respect your authority and, as an extension, honor and respect others. Rightly understood, good manners and proper social etiquette toward others is a barometer of an effective foundation for cultural survival. Where good manners and etiquette exist social interactions are elevated. Where good manners and social etiquette disappear, all manner of rudeness and even hostility arise. Gregg Jackson has given us a good primer to reclaim the lost territory in our social interactions today."

Pastor Mike Spaulding, Pastor of Calvary Chapel Lima and host of "Soaring Eagle Radio"

"As a father of ten, including four boys, *40 Rules to Help Boys Become Men* is a must-purchase for my kids. It was a very good read for me, too, helping restore some authentic chivalry that has been eroded in my own life from interaction with our increasingly debased culture. Based upon the principles of God's Word and our Christian heritage, *40 Rules to Help Boys Become Men* is a great companion to Scripture in the discipleship of the boys in your home. Wives and mothers, are you discouraged by the rude words and careless behavior from your husband and your kids? Buy this book and put it where they will see it. It will grab their attention, keep them reading, and by God's grace, help change them for the better."

Dr. Patrick Johnston, Director, Assn. of Pro-Life Physicians, Producer, *The Reliant,* and Author, *The Revolt of 2020, Body By Blood,* and *The Reliant*

"Gregg Jackson's, *40 Rules to Help Boys Become Men* will help parents to fulfill the charge in Ephesians 6:4 on raising children: 'Bring them [children] up in the culture [paidea] of the Lord.' Christianity is a lifestyle for families to practice, as well as a message to believe: 'Be on the alert, stand firm in the faith, act like men, be strong.' (I Corinthians 16:13). Gregg's book can benefit parents who desire to see their sons rebuild our culture through manhood. As a father of three adult sons, I highly recommend this book."

E. Ray Moore, Chaplain (Lt.Col) USAR, Ret. and Founder of Exodus Mandate Project

40 rules

to help **boys**
become **men**

**the lost arts
of manners
etiquette
+ behavior**

best-selling author

gregg jackson

Contents

Dedication xiii

Introduction xv

Foreword xvii

1   Open and close doors for women and elders...................... 1

2   Pull out chairs for women.. 2

3   Stand up when a woman or elders enter a room
or sit at a table. 3

4   Don't interrupt when others are talking............................... 4

5   Disagree without being disagreeable................................... 5

6   Don't talk back to parents, elders or teachers.
Show proper respect for authority. 7

7   Make eye contact when shaking hands and always
extend a firm hand. 8

8   Have a cheerful attitude when doing chores or work
of any kind. 9

9   Put your napkin on your lap before eating. 10

10   Keep your room neat and organized. 11

11   Wait for everyone to be seated before eating. 13

12   Chew with your mouth closed.. 14

13   Don't lie, steal or cheat. 15

14   Say "please" and "thank you."... 16

15   Take pride in your appearance.
"ALG" (Always Look Good). 17

16   Clear dishes without being asked...................................... 19

17   Leave a room you are in neater than when you found it..... 20

18   Say "excuse me" when others are speaking or when
walking in front of somebody... 21

19   Answer "yes sir" or "yes ma'am" whenever your parents
ask you to do something. Never complain. 22

20   Say "may I" (as opposed to "can I.")................................. 23

21   Help your parents around the house when they are
doing work... 25

22   Ask permission when in doubt. 26

23   Keep negative opinions to yourself.................................... 27

24   Don't comment on other people's physical appearance
unless you are complimentary. 28

25   Rather than talk about oneself, ask others how they are
doing. Take a sincere interest in the lives of others. 29

26   Cover your mouth when coughing or sneezing and
never pick your nose.. 31

27   Make good choices when posting to social media
and on the internet.. 32

28   Never use foul language.. 33

29   Even if bored at a performance or event, sit quietly and
patiently until it is over. 34

30   Thank your friends' parents when spending time
at their home. 35

31   Guard your eyes and ears... 37

32   Never call adults by their first name. Use proper respect
for elders and call them "Mr. (last name of the person)"
or "Mrs. (last name of the person)". 38

33   Put all electronics down when interacting with others........ 39

34   Ask to be excused from the table...................................... 40

35   Wash your hands thoroughly with soap before eating
and after going to the bathroom... 41

36   Choose Your Friends Wisely.. 43

37   Don't gossip or keep secrets about others........................ 44

38   Don't slouch in your chair... 45

39   Remove your jacket and hat before eating. 46

40   Keep your promises. Your word means everything............ 47

Dedication

This book is dedicated to the 2 best mothers in the world: Jill Jackson, my mom, and Annie Jackson, my wife of 20 years.

Mom, thanks for teaching me many of the basic manners and rules of etiquette in this book. I'm still working on many of them, but appreciate your persistent efforts in my formative years. The foundation you helped build in my life has been an enormous blessing.

Annie, thank you for diligently teaching them to our son Jake. I love you more than words can express.

Introduction

If you are reading these words you must be acutely aware that there has been a massive decline in basic manners and civility in our country. Many of the basic rules of manners and etiquette used to be passed down from parents to their children through the generations. But it seems that this practice has skipped the past few decades. These days, if a man holds open a door for a woman he may be called a misogynist. Nevertheless, if our nation is ever to become good again I believe it must start with us as parents in our own homes. I believe that we as parents have a duty to pass on to our progeny the basic manners and rules of etiquette that Scottish writer Alexander McCall Smith referred to as "the basic building blocks of civil society." That is exactly what I have endeavored to do with this little book. My hope and prayer is that a significant segment of this current generation of young boys, young adults, and subsequent generations will adopt these basic manners and rules of etiquette to help restore the civility, morality, decency and courtesy in America that was once commonplace.

Foreword

By Douglas J. Hagmann

Supreme Court Justice Clarence Thomas is quoted: "Good manners will open doors that the best education cannot." In his latest work, Gregg Jackson provides real-life direction that will not just open doors, but expand the entrances and illuminate the pathways to life's greatest opportunities.

Gregg Jackson's latest work functions as a logical follow-up to his previous book, "40 Things to Teach Your Children Before You Die," itself a valuable treasure of "simple" yet frequently elusive truths that provide a sound foundation of wisdom and Christian values. Building upon a solid bedrock of lessons that will serve a lifetime, Gregg's latest missive serves as a force majeure for young men and their mentors as a battle for character, integrity and honor rages.

Such battle lines have long been drawn, although they have been breached and reshaped in the first decades of this century by those who want to redefine civility and morality. Manners, etiquette and behavior that build and showcase character and integrity are being demonized as a tactic in this larger war against Biblical principles instilled by scripture.

Despite being engaged in this epic battle, direction from the pulpits and most of today's Christian pastors and ministers is uncommon. To provide such Biblical guidance, particularly to boys and young men is to invite calls of intolerance and bias. Attributes that define our character and morality are under assault through the perversity of Progressiveness. Such principles are under constant ridicule by cultural indoctrination antithetical to sound Biblical instruction.

Accordingly, a primer or playbook is needed to assist in the recalibration of our moral and spiritual compass to realign with Biblical scripture. It is therefore my honor to introduce Gregg Jackson's "40 Rules to Help Boys Become Men."

The effectiveness of Gregg Jackson's latest work is achieved and even amplified by its compendious format. He wastes no words to furnish a specific battle plan necessary to reclaim the fundamental Christian principles that are specific to young men.

Copies of Gregg Jackson's "40 Things to Teach Your Children Before You Die" can be found attached to my estate papers with specific instructions to my grandchildren upon my death, and have been given to each parent for their immediate guidance. Now, "40 Rules to Help Boys Become Men" has been added, for the greatest gift one can leave is one of rich instruction that outlives its sender.

1

Open and close doors for women and elders.

When you are entering or leaving a building, store, home, or even an elevator, always be aware of who is behind you and hold open the door for others before you enter or exit.

2

Pull out chairs for women.

Whether a meal takes place at home or in a restaurant, be sure to pull out any chairs for a woman sitting down. If there are multiple women, pull out the chair for the eldest and others if you are able to. When they are seated, help push their chair in toward the table.

3

Stand up when a woman or elders enter a room or sit at a table.

It is always a good show of respect to stand up when women or adults enter a room, especially if they are guests in your home. This doesn't necessarily apply to family members, but it does apply to guests and elders at home or in any social situation.

4

Don't interrupt when others are talking.

When others are talking, focus to the best of
your ability on what they are saying and make
sure you pause for a few seconds before
responding to ensure they are finished speaking.
Interrupting others is rude and demonstrates a
lack of respect for the person who is speaking.

5

Disagree without being disagreeable.

It is ok to disagree, but it is vital that you disagree without being arrogant or rude. Acknowledge what the other person is saying and respond with, "I hear what you are saying, but I have a different opinion. Would you mind if I share why?" or something similar.

6

Don't talk back to parents, elders or teachers. Show proper respect for authority.

In general, you should always obey your parents, teachers, and elders. However, if you disagree with what you are being asked to do, you should always respectfully acknowledge what is being asked of you and ask for further clarification. Never mumble under your breath, roll your eyes, or talk back in an insolent manner. Adults, especially your parents, are to be treated with the utmost respect.

7

Make eye contact when shaking hands and always extend a firm hand.

First impressions matter even more than you think. When you meet somebody for the first time, smile, extend your hand and shake hands with a good firm handshake. Tell the person, "it's nice to meet you" or "it's nice to see you again." Never look down or look away from the person. That eye-contact is important and helps establish trust.

8

Have a cheerful attitude when doing chores or work of any kind.

Doing chores or work around the house is not meant to be fun. If it were it wouldn't be called "work." ☺ However, work is a reality of life, and you will spend most of your life doing work of some kind. Knowing that is the case, you are in charge of the type of attitude you bring to your work. If you have a positive attitude, the work will get done faster and won't seem like so much of a burden.

9

Put your napkin on your lap before eating.

The first thing you should always do when sitting down to eat is put your napkin on your lap. It's good manners and also protects your pants from getting stained by any food that misses your mouth or accidentally falls off your plate or fork.

10

Keep your room neat and organized.

Make your bed neatly every morning and pick up all items off the floor. Like your appearance, your room says a lot about you. If it is neat and organized, it shows that you respect your parents and that, most likely, you are neat and organized as well.

11

Wait for everyone to be seated before eating.

Whether at home, somebody else's home or in a restaurant, it's always polite and consistent with good manners to stand behind your seat and wait to sit down until everyone is seated, especially women and elders.

12

Chew with your mouth closed.

Nobody wants to see the food in your mouth. When you are eating, always chew your food thoroughly and with your mouth closed. This means no talking while you are chewing. Also, try not to ask questions of anybody else while they are chewing or getting ready to chew.

13

Don't lie, steal or cheat.

These go without saying. Be honest and
straightforward to the best of your ability in
all your dealings and associations. Don't take
things that don't belong to you and always play
by the rules.

14

Say "please" and "thank you."

These simple words will get you far in life. It's amazing how many people these days don't say "please" and "thank you." You almost can't say them enough. They show respect to the person with whom you are speaking and are not referred to as "magic words" for nothing. Also, whenever you receive a gift make sure that you write a hand written thank you letter or card to the person who gave you the gift. It will take more time than sending an e-mail or text message but will demonstrate a lot more thought.

15

Take pride in your appearance. "ALG" (Always Look Good).

Always try to look your best. Your appearance says a lot about who you are. Brush your teeth, comb your hair and make sure you tuck in your shirt and dress up for school, church, going out to dinner and all other social occasions.

16

Clear dishes without being asked.

Chances are your mom or dad worked hard to prepare the meal you just ate. So, one great way to demonstrate your gratitude is to say thank you for preparing such a delicious meal and begin clearing the dishes when everyone is finished.

17

Leave a room you are in neater than when you found it.

This goes for every room that you are ever in. If you are on the couch, make sure that you neaten it up before leaving the room. If you are in the kitchen and notice some dishes in the sink, take the initiative to clean them even if they are not yours.

18

Say "excuse me" when others are speaking or when walking in front of somebody.

If you have to interrupt a conversation, it's always good manners to say, "excuse me for interrupting."

19

Answer "yes sir" or "yes ma'am" whenever your parents ask you to do something. Never complain.

It's not easy being a kid and chances are your parents ask you to do quite a bit. But they have your best interests at heart. Give your parents the benefit of the doubt and show them proper respect by always saying "yes, sir" or "yes, ma'am" when they request your help around the house. They will appreciate it and you will demonstrate your love and respect for them.

20

Say "may I" (as opposed to "can I.")

If you want to go outside and play, for example, you would ask "May I go outside and play?" verses "Can I go outside and play?" "May I" is proper English.

21

Help your parents around the house when they are doing work.

When you see your mom or dad doing work around the house, always ask them if you can help them in any way. They will appreciate it even if they say no. It demonstrates thoughtfulness and respect for your parents.

22

Ask permission when in doubt.

If you are in any doubt as to whether your parents will allow you to do something, always ask them. It is much better to hear them say no than to get in trouble in the future for doing something for which you should have asked permission.

23

Keep negative opinions to yourself.

There is a time and place for sharing negative opinions. However, in general, you should keep them to yourself and have as positive an outlook possible to the best of your ability.

24

Don't comment on other people's physical appearance unless you are complimentary.

It's always rude to make fun of other people whether in regard to their physical appearance or the way they are dressed. Try not to judge people by their outward appearance. Instead, try to appreciate them for who they are as a person, and not focus on temporal attributes that will pass away.

25

Rather than talk about oneself, ask others how they are doing. Take a sincere interest in the lives of others.

An important part of good manners is asking others how they are doing in their lives when they ask you how you are doing. Nobody likes a person who goes on and on about themselves never showing interest in others. Take the time to really get to know and understand the people with whom you come in contact in life.

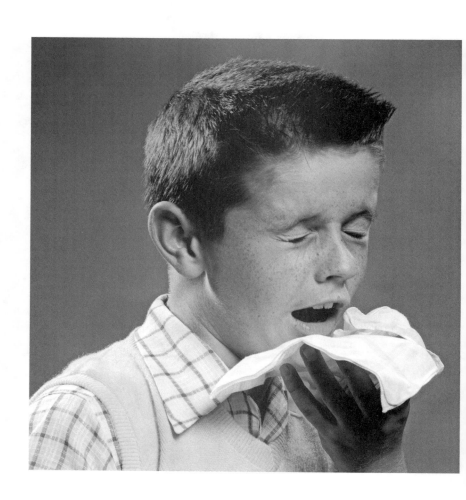

26

Cover your mouth when coughing or sneezing and never pick your nose.

If you cough or sneeze say, "excuse me" and try to wash your hands if possible. Moreover, if you feel something in your nose, blow your nose into a tissue.

27

Make good choices when posting to social media and on the internet.

If you wouldn't want it said about you or a loved
one, you shouldn't be posting it about others.
Plus these choices you make now will affect
you well into the future since once something
is posted online, even if you remove it,
it can live on forever.

28

Never use foul language.

While you may hear others use foul language, you should try to keep your language as clean as possible. The words you use reveal a lot about you. Use words that lift others up and encourage them. Foul "4 letter words" don't lift up and encourage and they usually demonstrate a deficient vocabulary, general ignorance and lack of class.

29

Even if bored at a performance or event, sit quietly and patiently until it is over.

Sometimes you will find yourselves in situations with grown-ups where the subject of the conversation or event you are at may be totally boring to you. However, it is always good manners to patiently endure with as positive an attitude as you can muster. Your parents most likely recognize the fact that the conversation or event is of little interest to you but will certainly appreciate the fact that you chose to not complain.

30

Thank your friends' parents when spending time at their home.

When you are at a friend's house, always show good respect to their parents by extending a friendly smile and handshake with solid eye contact. And thank them for having you as a guest in their home.

31

Guard your eyes and ears.

If your friends look at dirty pictures or videos,
talk about sexual things, or try to touch your
private parts, tell them it is wrong and get away
from them immediately. Also, tell your parents.
They have a right to know if your companions
are a threat to your purity. Many children have
been abused because they were either afraid to
walk away from sexual conversation and acts, or
afraid to tell their parents.

32

Never call adults by their first name. Use proper respect for elders and call them "Mr. (last name of the person)" or "Mrs. (last name of the person)".

Some of your friends may refer to adults by their first names, but you should always demonstrate proper respect for authority by referring to adults by their last name. It is good manners and will distinguish you from a lot of your peers.

33

Put all electronics down when interacting with others.

When speaking with others or being spoken to, put aside all technology whether it be a computer, tablet or smart phone. It is always rude to be on technology when interacting with others.

34

Ask to be excused from the table.

It's always rude to abruptly leave the table after eating, but if you have to prior to everyone else being finished, always ask, "may I be excused from the table?"

35

Wash your hands thoroughly with soap before eating and after going to the bathroom.

We wash our hands not only for our own health but also for the health of others, so we never want to handle any food with dirty hands. Always wash with warm water and scrub thoroughly with soap for at least 15 seconds. If possible dry your hands with a towel or dry cloth. They are superior to hand dryers for removing all bacteria. If using a public restroom, open the door handle with a paper towel to keep from contaminating your hands with the germs of others who don't wash their hands after going to the bathroom.

36

Choose Your Friends Wisely.

The Bible says, "bad company corrupts good character." Indeed, this is true. If you surround yourself with pessimistic, cynical people of low moral character then you are more likely to adopt their attitudes and behaviors. Therefore, choose your friends wisely and to the best of your ability limit your group of friends to those who encourage you and share your core values and beliefs.

37

Don't gossip or keep secrets about others.

Try never to talk behind other's backs. Unless it is positive, you are actually harming the person about whom you are talking. Plus they don't have the chance to defend themselves. To the best of your ability, be straightforward with people always speaking the truth in love.

38

Don't slouch in your chair.

Sit upright with your back straight. People don't respect a slouch who looks lazy and uninterested in what's going on around him. Plus it's bad for your posture.

39

Remove your jacket and hat before eating.

It's always rude to eat with your hat on. Remove it and set it aside prior to eating.

40

Keep your promises. Your word means everything.

If you make a commitment, keep it. This applies even if the commitment is small. You are what you actually do. Make a habit of following through on all the commitments you make to people and it will become a practice that will serve you well the rest of your life. People with integrity keep their promises to others.

"For God so loved the world, He gave His only Begotten Son that whosoever would believe in Him would not perish but have eternal life."
(John 3:16)